OLYMPIC BUTTER GOLD

Olympic Butter Gold

POEMS

Jonathan Moody

TriQuarterly Books/Northwestern University Press
Evanston, Illinois

TriQuarterly Books
Northwestern University Press
www.nupress.northwestern.edu

Printed in the United States of America

10 9 8 7 6 5 4 3 2 1

ISBN-13: 978-0-8101-3222-1 (paper)
ISBN-13: 978-0-8101-3223-8 (e-book)

Library of Congress Cataloging-in-Publication data are available from the Library of Congress.

for Shadé,

Avery Langston Erumuse,

3935,

& Hip-Hop

Contents

Acknowledgments   *ix*

Opening Ceremony
Chasing the American Dream   *7*

Freistil Battle
Son of a   *11*
Die Fantastischen Vier   *13*
Okaloosa County   *15*
Operation Just Cause, 1989   *16*
Paper Shredding Blues   *17*
Deployed   *19*
Mr. Señor Love Daddy   *21*
Telecommunications Act of 1996, or Ode to Black Radio   *24*
Improvisational Riff   *27*
Dancing with James Brown   *29*

Hip-Hop Saudade (Sho Nuff!)
Bricolage   *33*
Hip-Hop Nostaljack   *35*
The Low End Theory   *37*
Berry Gordy's *The Last Dragon*   *38*
Luke Cage, Hip-Hop Superhero for Hire   *40*
John Stewart, the Black Green Lantern, Drops Science with Defiance   *41*
What's Beef: The Unauthorized Biography of Dr. John Henry Irons's
     Alter Ego, Steel   *43*

Lovelust à la Mode
Supersonic   *47*
Tough Love   *48*
B-Boy Manifesto   *49*

Manhattan   *50*

Lovelust à la Mode   *51*

Spawn   *53*

Paranoid   *55*

The Making of a Fresno, Texas, Love Poem   *56*

Chorophobia   *57*

Olympic Butter Gold (United States East Coast Interlude)   *58*

Regularizer (**The G-Funk Semi-Finals**)

Portrait of Hermes as a B-Boy   *61*

Sticky Icky Icky   *63*

Kleosphobia   *65*

Choppin'   *66*

Ersatz   *67*

The Thief's Theme   *69*

Dear 2Pac,   *71*

Regulate   *73*

Ronda Final (**Awready**)

OutKast Crown   *77*

Unsung   *81*

Houston   *82*

Olympic Butter Gold (Havana, Cuba, Interlude)   *83*

Hip-Hop   *84*

Pintata   *85*

2084 (From Ghetto Fabulous to Ghetto Fascist)   *86*

2Pac Pantoum   *88*

2084 (Remix)   *90*

Gothic Barkley   *91*

Notes   *93*

Acknowledgments

Grateful acknowledgment is made to the editors of the following publications, in which these poems first appeared (sometimes in a different version):

Beloit Poetry Journal: "Olympic Butter Gold (United States East Coast Interlude)"

Borderlands: Texas Poetry Review: "Houston"

The Common: "Paranoid," "Chorophobia," "Portrait of Hermes as a B-Boy," "Kleosphobia," and "Dear 2PAC,"

Houston Chronicle: "Tough Love"

It Was Written: Poetry Inspired by Hip-Hop: "Die Fantastischen Vier"

joINT. Literary Magazine: "Chasing the American Dream," "Supersonic," and "Mr. Señor Love Daddy"

Tattoosday: "Spawn"

The Southern Poetry Anthology, VIII: Texas (Huntsville: Texas Review Press, 2015): "Unsung"

Tidal Basin Review: "Deployed," "Luke Cage, Hip-Hop Hero for Hire," "John Stewart, the Black Green Lantern, Drops Science with Defiance," "The Unauthorized Biography of John Henry Irons (aka Steel)," and "2084 (From Ghetto Fabulous to Ghetto Fascist)"

Xavier Review: "Berry Gordy's *The Last Dragon*"

"Manhattan" was broadcast on KUHA's *Front Row* (91.7 FM, Houston).

"The Thief's Theme" appears in the *2013 Houston Poetry Fest Anthology*.

"Gothic Barkley" appears on Friendswood Public Library's online blog, *from the reference desk*.

Thanks to the literary communities of New Orleans, Pittsburgh, and Houston for showing me mad love during the initial and intermediate stages of my development as a poet.

A special shout-out goes to Cave Canem. Big ups to Amanda Johnston. Crazy love goes to Tyehimba Jess for volunteering to read one of my earlier manuscripts without my having to ask him. Adrian Matejka and Roger Reeves, good looking out. Much respect to my big brothers: James Cagney and Myron Michael. I also want to thank Major Jackson and Terrance Hayes for inspiring me to take my writing seriously. Cornelius Eady and Toi Derricotte, thanks for your vision.

Shout-out to Dr. Biljana Obradovic for still holding it down at Xavier University of Louisiana's creative writing department and to the Pitt MFA program and its alumni for making major moves. Got to give it up for my Pittsburgh peeps Kris Collins and Scott Silsbe for their continued friendship and support over the years; the former played a huge role in getting my first book published, but he'll be quick to downplay it.

Thanks to Dr. John Gorman and Dr. Rekha Subramanian for allowing me to get my shine on at UH–Clear Lake's Open Mic Reading Series. Shout-out to *Public Poetry.* One love to Stephen Gros, Joe B., and Zelene Pineda Suchilt for spearheading Houston's Word Around Town (WAT) Poetry Tour. Props to the WAT veterans and the current poets in the lineup who keep me on my toes. Shout-out to Lupe and Jasminne Mendez. 'Nuff respect to Winston Derden for helping me revise "Operation Just Cause, 1989" and for creating *Speak!Poet.* Chris Wise, thanks for being the greatest hype man and storyteller I've ever met.

I can't forget Malik JoDavid Sales, Chris Buckley, Paul Lee, and Uncle Melvin; I have enjoyed our countless conversations about the state of rap music.

Props to Parneshia Jones and Frank X. Walker for selecting my manuscript. Thanks to the entire sales and marketing team at Northwestern University Press.

Extended thanks to Pearland High School (especially to the English department and to my past and current students).

One love to my in-laws repping "Mo City," Texas, to the fullest, to my Alabama and Georgia fam, and to my folks still holding it down in Fort Walton Beach, Florida.

R.I.P. to my Choctawhatchee High School classmate Shane Gibson (1979–2014), the legendary guitarist who shredded for Korn after the departure of Brian "Head" Welch.

R.I.P. to my Choctawhatchee High School classmate Sam Hairston (1979–2014), a devoted husband, father, and soldier who was killed in action in Ghazni, Afghanistan.

R.I.P. to my cousin Tommy Lee Howard (1956–2013), who toughened me up by fouling the hell out of me every time I took the ball to the hole.

OLYMPIC BUTTER GOLD

If there was a HIP-HOP or Rap Olympics, I really don't think the United States would get Gold, Silver or Brass . . . —CHUCK D

Politics in any country in the world is dangerous . . . politics had better be disguised as poetry. —LANGSTON HUGHES

Opening Ceremony

Chasing the American Dream

Every time
I hold
my rusty spoon

above the Statue
of Liberty's torch,
I struggle to find a vein.

Freistil Battle

Son of a

after Camp Lo

I am the son of DJ Kool
Her-Her-Her-Her Herc,

weighing in at two turntables
& a microphone

Son of a goatskin drum
speaking patois

Son of a dub instrumental
keeping uptown rockers

jamming in Jah's presence:
Ahah ah ah ahhh Ahah ah ah

Baby I . . . am the unfortunate son
of the Cross Bronx Expressway

that displaced poor blacks
& Latinos to East Brooklyn

Son of a B-Girl's
neon acrylic fingernail

Son of a milk crate loaded
with nickel bags of funk

Son of the soap suds
making-out on stoop steps

Son of the Afro pick
with the black fist handle grip

Son of the MAC-11, 32-round
mag & sound suppressor

Son of a wire tap
Son of a billy club

Son of blunt force trauma
to the back of the skull

Son of the steam iron drying out
blood money tossed in the toilet

Son of an unlocked fire hydrant
cooling off scorching crime waves

Son of a B-side single
still in heavy rotation

Son of the cross-fader
mixing disco with krautrock.

Die Fantastischen Vier

I made loot on the side teaching
Germans at Rhein-Mein Air Base
the art of B-Boying. Benjamin
always brought Kurtis Blow's
"The Breaks" to every lesson,
& the staccato breakdown
of steel drums, which invited
average B-Boys to bust six-step
downrocks, was a pair of rapidly
twirling ropes that made Benjamin
freeze up harder than Ms. Krause's
Kool Kups. "Maybe I should break
to 'Apache'?" Jürgen swore he was down
by law to rep Frankfurt to the fullest
& saved Benjamin from further shame:
"Nein, quit being such a dick shit.
Incredible Bongo Band would make
you have heart attack." "How 'bout ESG's
'UFO'?" Ursula asked. Her suggestion,
as bright as her blonde streaks.
In rhythm to the bass, drums,
& sparse guitar lick, Benjamin spun
his body around slowly like the 12"
vinyl rotating on Ursula's turntable.
He was a spacecraft rotating
over the cardboard rug of my basement.
Jürgen, who inched toward the center
popping & locking, retreated
when Benjamin became a spinning
top; he whirled so fast he turned

himself upside down & continued
twirling on his blue Kangol.
Hip-hop witnessed a dude
with two left Adidas shoes become
kinship spirit with the music.

Okaloosa County

In Fort Walton Beach,
FL, Mama's house rattles
from the aftermath
of daisy cutters

dropping on an Eglin
Air Force Base test range;
her military retirement
check can't cover

the cost it takes to replace
shattered windows.
& You can catch the FDLE's Sex
Offender Database turbo-charging

lies to boost the engine
of tourism. At Mr. J's
Barbershop, the baby boomers
could care less about voting

but sport star-spangled
doo rags & take pride
in "Air" Jordan's Olympic
butter gold dunk

courtesy of Magic's
no-look, behind-
the-back cinnamon
apple pie dish.

Operation Just Cause, 1989

On my nightstand, the empty rocket
casing used in Panama chilled—
a hand-me-down gift from
my father's friend. "This baby
here & the South Florida Drug Task,"
he said, "played a part in containing drugs."

In our fridge, there were mad
drugs in rocket-shaped bottles
more advanced than the one in my room.

My father's medicine, muzzled
with bottle caps, maintained high velocity,
penetrating cells in his brain.
I grew tired of collecting discarded
casings among the ruins of smashed
dinner plates. When I intervened
on behalf of his liver,
he sucked his teeth & reloaded.

"She turned you against me,"
he said in excuse for the destruction.

Mama's status switching
from acquaintance to nemesis,
hella faster than I could say *Noriega*.

Paper Shredding Blues

the speaker is a paper shredder

I'm tired of shredding incriminating evidence;
the number of strips my owner carries

to the dumpster should equal the number
of years he'd face in prison. My mind

bleeding green with names
of military personnel & federal agents

who've discussed drug shipment
updates like the latest box scores.

All those destroyed families. Those burgeoning
revolutions, pacified. Another document,

force-fed into my mouth.
I'm supposed to be fasting.

I've already forgotten the names that grace
the front because my working memory

is an unpaid intern with little ambition.
Can only consume so much. But this arrogant

man believes I can keep pace. Why wouldn't he?
My cross-cut shredder tears paper

into bits the way stomach enzymes
break down protein. Through all the confusion,

he's convinced that sending drugs to Miami, New York City,
Detroit, Chicago, Houston, L.A., & D.C. is a necessary evil.

To help fund covert operations. To sedate
the consciousness of inner-city youths

& turning Brother against Brother: more proof
corroborating his main point—that greater police

presence is required in the hood. My power cord
is a tail longing to trip his secretary:

so hard that when she hits the floor, face down,
her purple pumps pop off & reveal gaping holes

at the bottom of her stockings—gaping holes mirroring
what our Society sorely lacks: support.

Deployed

One time for the bald eagle perched
on crony capitalism's hairy mole.

Two times for idle moving vans
& their mounted backscatter

X-ray scanners inspecting
my khakis for dub sacks.

Three times for GPS tracking
devices on the ashy ankles of truant

teens. Four times for the NSA
pecking through the eggshell

of our Fourth Amendment.
Five times for the whistle

water tubing on Snowden's saliva.
Six times for government heads

& intelligence agencies
forgetting to change the sheets

after secret affairs.
Seven times for Gil Scott-

Heron & Goodie Mob.
Eight times for counter

surveillance cameras
detecting rifle scopes

aimed at innocent B-Boys.
Nine times for the 9th Circuit

Court of Appeals for allowing
the government to keep a digital eye

on every keystroke I make. Ten times
for brothers everywhere cracking CODESPEAK.

Mr. Señor Love Daddy

a character from Spike Lee's Do the Right Thing

I've seen a WMD
without a brain. But never
a brain without a WMD.

SUPPORT OUR ~~TROOPS~~
& get knuck if you buck?

Don't they know no good?
oughta be ashamed
of earwigging on trash talk,

of implanting biochips
while sizing up likelihoods

of disco ballers prone
to praising Allah,
of whether Aim

toothpaste has financed
hijackers under the sink?

Ain't that some messed up ish?
Don't it make you wanna lash out
& pick fights with strobe lights?

Well, pump your fists
in the air. Wave 'em

Like you just don't care. If your
tv set preaches Armageddon,
let me hear you say: *Oh yeah!*

And for the Johnny-Come-Lately
just tuning in—who ain't hip

to the haps—we've been
rendered impotent for
"the good of the masses."

Crap game alert.
Crap game alert:

the more you chill in the streets,
the more digital photos they'll
compile of us in suspect files.

*And really, who gives a damn
if Bert & Ernie get hitched?*

*What them muthasuckas do during
commercials is they own gotdam
bizness! And that's the truth, Ruth!*

You've been cold lamping
here on WE LOVE RADIO,

108 FM on your dial.
This is ya Mr. Señor Love Daddy
talking while they stalking.

Wanna send this Roy Ayers vibe
out to Big L, Big Pun, Aaliyah, Left Eye,

Jam Master Jay, ODB, Luther Vandross, J. Dilla,
James Brown, Pimp C, Michael Jackson, Isaac Hayes,
G.U.R.U., Nate Dogg, Heavy D, Whitney Houston, MCA,

Bobby "Blue" Bland, Donna Summer, Donald Byrd,
Nelson Mandela, Ossie Davis, & Ruby Dee. We miss y'all.

Telecommunications Act of 1996, or Ode to Black Radio

for Amiri Baraka

The ban on the number of stations
                companies could own
was lifted like an arrest warrant.

                        Corporate execs stocked up
                                as, as, as if H.A.A.R.P.'s
                        extremely low frequencies
                                would alter the ionosphere
                        & trigger hurricanes
                                dropping harder
                        than killer remixes.

San Antonio took the lead.
                Clear Channel cleared
away any chance for unsigned
                hypes to get props,
for black intellectuals
                to politic on the Sirius B tip.

                        Here is somethin' ya can't understand:

                        years later, Disney deciding it's *tuh time for*
                                some/ time for some action. $96 mill to kill
                        2 black rivals. *One Family, One Station*
                                strong-arming *The Tom Joyner Morning*
                        Show to kiss KISS-FM good-bye.

Black radio's a frog; all it wants
          Erykah Badu
        is *your ka-ka-ka-ka-ka-ka kiss*
to become Prince Nelson again.

                Live dialectical discourse on mandatory
                    minimums, shunted by voice-tracked
                deejays airing prerecorded banter

                  about the fishnet dress hugging
                Kim Kardashian's post-baby body.

Yes, yes, y'all:
          Clinton tied Revolution's brass balls
to Newton's cradle—
        only way rebellion gains
momentum is if it's confined to a pendulum.

Not the first time he hypnotized folks.
          With his sultry sax,
he riffed Razorback showmanship
            & took the *Arsenio Hall Show*
to commercial as soon as black ballots
          landed at his feet like sheer petal thongs.

Black radio's a frog; all it wants
          Erykah Badu *is your extra time.*

Until that golden nugget of a moment
          figures out how to unlock the vault
from inside, amphibious talking heads
          will remind listeners
to drink Bud Light Lime responsibly

         & that local artists can gain airplay
as long as their trap beats
         as long as their trap beats
as long as their trap beats
         make Homicide
outline Bankruptcy in chalk.

Improvisational Riff

the speaker is Arsenio Hall

Yo, Premier, give me a collard
greens, chitlins, leftover meatloaf beat

with plenty of Diana Ross supreme
ketchup wrapped in a buttermilk mothership

that flew first-class from North Cackalack
to Cali & some cinnamon soil fudge

preheated to hot comb Fahrenheit.
Yes, yes, give me a break beat so nasty

it'll synchronize the monthly cycles
of every B-Girl in the world

& catch Yosemite Sam & Bugs
Bunny in a compromising position.

Give me a beat filled with fault line funk
turning Rip Van Winkle into a rap insomniac.

I want to hear those subwoofers
thu-thump, thump a Tell Tale heartbeat

that effs with Mel Gibson's conscience.
I want a harmony so raw it'll shut

down Spike Lee's Knickerbocker
trash talk—make Celtics fans

eat a leprechaun's
botanical boogers.

Dancing with James Brown

We pivot off the left heels
of silver-sequined shoes,
spin 720°; our frames freeze
extinguishing Molotov cocktails.
Leaping over riot police,
The Hardest Working Man
in Show Business & I land
smoothly, do the splits above
the blue & red strobe lights
of squad cars. I draw both legs
back together, slowly crank
my body upright
as if my soul had a flat.
Goose bumps are pieces
of popcorn appearing
on Justice's flabby arms.
King James whips out a comb,
parts the black sea of his Afro,
& everyone living in America
watches Oscar Grant walk
to the mountaintop unscathed.

Hip-Hop Saudade (Sho Nuff!)

Bricolage

I.
On vinyl grooves,
a deejay's hands flashed
back & forth—built
a bridge of dialogue
between J.B.
& Jesse Jackson:
Guh guh guh-guh guh
Good Gawd,
Bruh bruh bruh-bruh
Bruthas & sistuhs,
the park was sanctuary—
fluid rhymes reduced
disco fever. B-Boys
held hands & caught
waves of energy
like the turntables plugged
into lampposts.

II.
Right arm parallel
to broken glass
& piss puddles,
one B-Boy carried
an imaginary umbrella.
His Jackie Wilson footwork,
creating the illusion
of powerful wind pulling
him back to charred

tenements while he stepped
forward towards
terraced townhouses.

III.

for Skeme
In a glowing ghost yard,
the little ball inside aerosol
cans bounced like gas
molecules. Ed Koch & his razor
wire, shaving peach fuzz
off of Notoriety's face,
couldn't stop prodigal
Picassos from hopping fences
& bombing blank
subway car canvasses.
Skeme-at-ic mist billowed
into a customized critique
contained in big block,
silver letters: ALL YOU SEE
IS CRIME IN THE CITY.

From the Boogie Down Bronx
to Manhattan, station agents
were de facto chief curators
who didn't trip
when homeless men
stood too close
to the masterpiece
'cause the poor were visibly
invisible like a graffiti
tagger's cryptic insignia.

Hip-Hop Nostaljack

I miss raw boom-bap.
Courageous cats
stepping into ciphers
& spitting fire
so blazing Evel Knivel
wouldn't come near it.

Can't forget ambiguous
graffiti font: how interlocked
S's, *T*'s, & *E*'s were arrows
pointing youngbloods
towards celebrity status—
their tagged, metallic canvases
passing through bodacious
bodega boroughs,

but I don't miss
Agent Orange's
toxic fumes:
stripped South Bronx's
ozone of oxygen molecules
the way it stripped
the leaves off trees
in Vietnam.

I miss KangaROOS shoes;
the zippered
side pocket
taught me the value
of a dollar.

I miss record needle
static, not the sound
of AIDS referred
to as "Gay Cancer."

I miss classic underground
shit that increased
my vocab & introduced
me to jazz.

The Low End Theory

kneaded tedious time

        effortlessly, without fail,

in half like dough—

        as my boom box inflated copyright claims:

my blank Memorex cassette

        high-speed dubbing sound—

feeding off a Native Tongues classic

        magnetically stripped—

authentic as sweet potato cornbread—

        scooped with a crochet kufi. Bro,

'Tip & Phife, far from sucker emcees, sifted

        their infinite stardust talent. Tribe bundled

rhythmic side dish of soulful sound—

        the dented can of their career—

loaded with okra & onions—

        its smudged expiration date, illegible.

Berry Gordy's *The Last Dragon*

Tight Buddha smoke curls & spirals
from blunts rolled longer than Kareem
Abdul-Jabbar's index finger, as Bruce Lee

connects a roundhouse kick to an enemy's
cheekbone on the big screen.

A myth flares up. It's about Leroy Green
catching bullets with his teeth! There's Sho Nuff.
The self-proclaimed Shogun of Harlem,

a kung fu warrior, the meanest, prettiest,
baddest mothersucker down around this town

standing taller than a tight end, an '80s
superhuman cool comic-book hybrid
of Jim Kelly & Jim Brown clad in black

shades, a fire-red samurai suit & football
pads. "Bruce" Leroy's the one who blocks

his path to supremacy, who won't flinch
from fists of fury barely brushing his brows,
who can make the loudmouth villain sit down

& shut up. But why does he dodge rivalry
& passion? Grasp chopsticks better than

the art of making love? Is catching a bullet
between his teeth deadlier than opening
a fortuneless fortune cookie?

It's 1985. I live in Frankfurt. My mother grounds
me. "No kung fu movies for eight weeks,"

she says. I used a punch-kick combo
to teach the 1st-grade bully a lesson, & made
him kiss the victim's lipstick-red Converse

to make amends. In real life, folks don't mess
with people their size, the bad guys seldom

go down, & the good ones get punished
for doing the right thing. There's no reward:
no Motown background music, no sultry

Siren beseeching you to guard her body,
or volunteering to "show you some moves,"

no sublime Glow outlining your skin
once you surpass martial arts' final level.
Instead, a black belt of discipline strikes

my bare bottom. My mother, wise as Confucius,
utters, "Learn the art of fighting without fighting."

Luke Cage, Hip-Hop Superhero for Hire

My indestructible skin resists the battering
ram of a fan's autograph request.

Diddy doesn't want what happened
to Biggie to happen to him.

Every move this bad boy
makes I counter like a chess piece

'cause any one of these neon lights
flashing from the DJ's booth

could be a tactical, green electro-
sight laser sizing up my client's torso.

Chillin' in the VIP section,
he fills up a glass with pineapple Ciroc

& nods his head to Cypress Hill's
"How I Could Just Kill a Man";

the tight waves in his freshly
cut fade are stenciled

in deep like letters on a tombstone.
It's my job to see death

in everything so Diddy
can enjoy life.

John Stewart, the Black Green Lantern,
Drops Science with Defiance

for M & F

Record labels insist trends can survive
the hard vacuum of space unprotected,

but Earth's atmosphere
distorts the industry's view

of Art. My green lantern's
light carries rap crews to remote

space stations where moguls
are devoted to developing music

& do not send artists
back down to Earth

for making ambitious
turns towards Mars.

This ring, the hip alien
named Afrika Bambaataa

bestowed upon me, summons
the intergalactic posse

of meteoroids to crush
Marketing: an evil force

more formidable than Sinestro.
5: radiant, 4: energy, 3: emanates,

2: from the ring's center, 1: light
goes *Zih Zih Zih Zih Zih*

preventing bionic brothers
from signing deals

that'll make debt skyrocket
faster than success.

What's Beef: The Unauthorized Biography of
Dr. John Henry Irons's Alter Ego, Steel

after The Notorious B.I.G.

Beef is when your weapons
prototypes are leaked

to engineer murders overseas
& genocidal gang violence.

Beef is when an innocent man
has to fake his own death,

switch names like license
plates, & escape to Metropolis.

Beef is when Lex Luthor
assumes you can't scrap

'cause you're a black "with
honors" graduate of Yale.

Beef is when Superman
suddenly saves your life

& says you need to *make*
your life *count for something*.

Beef is when Lois Lane
forgets about her exclusive

so she can be your voice
of reason. Beef is when

the lesser of two evils fronts
like it's the greater good.

Lovelust à la Mode

Supersonic

At Eglin Air Force Base, rumors
about my first girlfriend traveled
at the speed of sound. Some said
she kept emergency parachutes
in her purse because her hormones
would tail spin. Others believed
she was a crafty dope dealer
who flew under the radar.
On Beal Parkway, my mama's
white-diamond El Dorado
became a sailplane
sculpted by the Egyptian
god of wind & air. Rushed
to beat me home from school
only to catch footage
of Tipper Gore branding
a scarlet letter *E* for *Explicit*
across my girlfriend's breast.
Yes: my teenage love bounced
her booty like a subwoofer,
but she knew more about Africa
than my World History teacher.
"Is your girlfriend *also* the one who told
you that blacks were the first people
on Earth?" "Yes, ma'am."
"I need to speak with her parents."
"She doesn't know who her real
folks are. It's a toss-up
between Bessie Smith
& Charlie Parker, but she has more
godfathers than the Zulu Nation."

Tough Love

"Boy, just because your voice
is deeper than your father's

that don't make you
the man of the house,"

my mama said
after she slapped

me so hard my wisdom
teeth formed a union.

They sunk back into the gums
& refused to protrude

until I brought my temper
up to safety regulation standards.

B-Boy Manifesto

When the heart skips break
beats, B-Boys don't dance

around the turntable
of commitment.

Manhattan

for Shadé

My wife & I walk through the multihued
pinball machine that is Times Square.
In Manhattan, we're the only ones sober
& the bright lights think this is all gravy;
they never serve patrons water
after midnight but make an exception
because it's our first time in New York.
We raise our bottled beverages
& tap them in the air; the lust
in our eyes is more ravenous
than the homeless man filching
uncooked hot dogs from a vendor.
I grab my wife around the waist & kiss
her neck. In Manhattan, there's no
such thing as public displays of affection:
the more people we're surrounded
by the more alone we are—our heavy
breathing drowns out indie rock
blasting from a hipster's
luxury model beehive. My wife rests
both arms on my shoulders.
I caress her face; the loose eyelash
falling on my palm is a petal
meaning there's no chance in prolonging
the life of this moment. Holding hands,
we trudge towards the parking garage
ready to fill up our Cavalier's half-empty
tank with the honey on our lips.

Lovelust à la Mode

—and oh, the flowing of the honey, the paroxysms of joy,
hours and hours of coition. Equality!—ANAÏS NIN

. . . Even caramel sundaes is getting touched
Scooped in my ice cream truck, who tears it up?—METHOD MAN

for Shadé

It makes no sense paralleling
a hottie like yourself to a caramel sundae

because I am lactose intolerant. But I milk
every chance for you to be my cherry.

On top. You sweat beneath
whipped cream clouds

& smell like exotic desserts.
Let me soufflé your zesty pavlova

& turn your choco chip biscuits
upside down as I set the mood like a mawkish

mariachi playing "Guantanamera"
for Don Dadas who see emotions

as cactus worms & tequila,
embalming fluid.

My lips are poached
pears that have marinated in wine.

If Beyoncé & Hov were so turnt
that they blacked-out

after their midnight smash,
then we're Fresno, Texas's finest winos

wondering how in the hell
did we wind up in Fresno, Cali

cuffed to a French
bistro's front door.

Spawn

I came to Half Price Books
hoping to find hidden Todd McFarlane
gems in graphic novel bins,
but there were as many cop cars
behind my ride as there are traffic
lights in Fresno, Texas.

My fam told me that's how Pearland
police rolls: pulling
people over for driving three miles
above the speed limit; for not
signaling when switching lanes.

Green paint dripped
off my Chevy Caprice as if it melted
in the triple digit heat, but I was chill
until the white furry dice
dangling from the mirror reminded
me that Driving While Black was a gamble.

I'm a veteran actor. Spent
my whole career playing the role
of an innocent man who's convinced
himself he's done something wrong.
This scene, no different.
Only one take to look terrified
cops would discover Colombian
raw hidden beneath
the passenger seat.

My motivation: stay alive
& return home to my pregnant wife,
so I turned down the bass
& stopped rhyming
along with Chuck D.
Exercised the right to remain
quiet on the set.

Thought I was chill chill,
not the irredeemable
monster spawn who made
a deal in Hell so he could
come back to Earth & avenge
the deaths of defenseless people
whose lives were snuffed.

But I felt the six hour copacetic
cosmetics job it took for me
to look human became ruined
from the sweat trickling
down my forehead:
reasonable doubt that deep
inside I resembled
the irredeemable monster spawn
Society made me out to be.

Regrouped. Visualized
my Freedom scraping
against the coral reef of hard time.

Stuffed the license,
registration, & proof of insurance
into my smart mouth,
& feared my acting chops
would peel away like the dead
skin around my freshly
inked ankh.

Paranoid

I've passed down my fear
of the police to my baby boy
who always sleeps, frozen,
with his hands in the air.

Corralling around dancing
clouds, Lil' Bo Peep's
sheep wag their badges
behind them.

Avery Langston's
funky cold congestion,
probable cause
he's trafficking crack.

Lil' Bo Peep squeezes
air out of a blue bulb
& places the tip
at my son's left nostril;

the air coming back
pulls out nothing
but encrypted audio files
of my kisses good night.

The Making of a Fresno, Texas, Love Poem

After crickets complete their sound check,
our son's eyes drink light
coming from a news channel
broadcasting nothing but darkness.

The menthol scent of Aquaphor Healing
Ointment caked on his face can't mask
the Jealousy flooding our family room
like day-old fish grease coming to a boil.

Avery Langston lacks your high cheekbones,
narrow chin, & pouty lips,
but he's inherited your ability to smile
with ease: meaning when you disappear

to the kitchen to pump,
his face still holds your reflection
like a spoon we will one day use
to feed him carrots, apples, & parsnips.

Chorophobia

The night sky's crescent nose,
tailor-made for stirring

the punch bowl of spiked
gossip, spins De La Soul's "Buddy."

But my wife's fear of dancing
bumps the turntable.

"Baby, Cassiopeia ain't studdin'
you. She's too busy admiring

her freshly Botoxed face."
In one sparkly, pink

headphone bud out the other.
With my thumb, I trace a key

on Shadé's head & unlock
the brain region controlling

impulsive behavior.
My wife, afraid of falling

on her butt, can only curl
her hair while striking a pose

in the flamingo stance—the irony,
transparent like a silver wax LP.

Olympic Butter Gold (United States East Coast Interlude)

Olympic torch flamin', we burn so sweet
The thrill of victory, the agony, defeat—U GOD

the speaker is Fab 5 Freddy

MC Agent Orange, a former Chess prodigy,
likens his rapping style to a drunk

kung fu master: his unorthodox
cadences are purple centipedes

winding around grimy beats.
No Cuban Link, diamond-

studded Jesus piece—
just a wreath of firecrackers.

With a brown paper bag cloaked
over the mic, he steps to the stage

& chugs imaginary swigs
of truth serum. In the other

hand, a tray of horse mackerel
sushi & bluefin tuna

suggests he's about
to serve raw verses.

Regularizer (The G-Funk Semi-Finals)

Portrait of Hermes as a B-Boy

for Brian Johnson

To the tune of Can's "Vitamin C,"
I engage Soul Elemental
in an intense charades game
of knife-cutting gestures;
in the middle of the dance floor,
we Brooklyn Uprock,
in unison, facing opposite:
our shuffling feet & stabbing
motions approach each other
but never make contact.
He points at my half sister,
Aphrodite—the cascading stairs
leading to the bathroom—&—
pressing his tongue against the inside
of his cheek—pantomimes a blow job:
an unexpected B-Boy burn
expressing what went down
while I waited ages in a zigzag
mess to lay hands on the club's
finest bottle of coolie high harmony.
The news of Soul Elemental getting brain
while Aphrodite's entourage
of sparrows kept its eye
on the door carves a diagonal cut
from the cheekbone to the corner
of my mouth. Adding margarita salt
& lime juice to the wound,

Soul Elemental clips the wings
of my designer shell-toe Adidas,
but I, the O.G. psychopomp,
promptly provide him
safe passage through Hades.

Sticky Icky Icky

Raheem's weed dealer ran out of "AT&T"
        but insists his innovative strain,
"Andrew Aurenheimer,"

is A1 because it'll help
        us write THE poem
that'll capture the voice

of our generation, & I tell
        him my imagination weighs
a brick: worth as much

as the autographed Pippen
        jersey hanging above the fireplace's
nickel-layered arch front.

Cumulus clouds of dank
        smoke turn the combination
dials of Raheem's iron lungs

& lift the loot he owes.
        "Bro, didn't we just chop
it up about you robbing *Peter* Tosh

to pay *Paul* McCartney?"
        But he don't hear me
though; his mind travels

at 186,000 miles per second,
        "Yo, yo, yo, I've got a great
idea for a Jesse Jackson spoof

shirt: 'I AM SOMEBODY'S
      ONLY BLACK FRIEND.'"
30 shirt ideas later,

I wrap up Raheem's monologue
      in a big ball of foil.
On our way to Jack in the Box,

a cop hits me with a $500 fine
      for feeding
homeless veterans.

Kleosphobia

Inside Raheem's Windbreaker
jacket lining is a pair of Dwayne Wayne glasses
that would make his street cred plummet
like the Dow Jones, but his selective
intelligence manifests to point out how *nuptial*
is the feminine past participle of *nūbere*:
"to take a husband for every damn thing he's got.
Man, the moon's the nicest female in the galaxy,
but if she caught me cheating she'd walk away
with my Galveston sugar shack cottage
& the fucking Gulf of Mexico."
"But," I say, "she'd convince
herself that her constant phases
caused you to step out on y'all's marriage:
one quarter there's a shadow masking
her sociable side, & months later
she's an open-source satellite
tracking meteoroids of happiness.
All this to say that those hours spent
arguing over who'd keep
the rare Diabolical Biz Markie
Beat-Boxing Doll will seem pointless."

Choppin'

Yo Mama
so dumb when I asked

her to motorboat
me she demanded

to see my fishing
license.

Ersatz

Had I spotted D rocking
fake Pumas before we'd hiked
up the school stairs, we wouldn't
have had to lounge in the bathroom
during second period Bio.
"You trying to get dissected?
Genuine kicks don't come
with heel tags." D was too
concerned with what some
comedienne on HBO's
Def Comedy Jam had said
about his boo, Mary J. Blige:
how she needed to quit
regurgitating soulful classics
& bring an original cornbread
recipe to the grown folks' table.
"This'll cheer you up,"
Ryan said holding the latest
Playboy issue. "Bet
those big breastisis
would give me black eyes."
Anna Nicole Smith
was a Marilyn Monroe wannabe
who wouldn't be caught dead
reading *Ulysses* while perched
on a playground roundabout.
But to each his hormones.
While the call & response sounds
of Luke Campbell & the crowd

chanting *doo doo brown* escaped
my Walkman, the interim principal
stepped out of a stall. We didn't
sweat the demerits; we had
our parents' signatures down pat.

The Thief's Theme

Prometheus stole fire
from gods & gave

it to the humblest
homeboys.

If he pulled that stunt
today, disguised

as a fifteen-year-old
in skinny jeans

& black & white checkered
sneaks, he'd get called

The Flaming Faggot
as soon as he confessed

he was born in Greece
& had transferred

from an all-boy's school.
Criticized for his cluelessness

of *Maxim* magazine
& *Jersey Shore*,

for schooling Vegans
on how the moon

contains the healthiest
source of calcium.

Not designated Teacher's Pet
but a Teacher's Pet Peeve.

Kicked out of class for
trying to impress

the big-breasted
brunette

by lifting up his white
V-neck & showing

her the gaping hole
where his liver used to be.

Dear 2Pac,

I begin with Byron & Tennyson
               & watch my students bury
their heads on desks; they rest

easier than the deceased.
               Dear 2Pac, it's me against
the world of indifference.

I display your photo on the projector:
               your arms tatted up; your iced-out-
diamond DEATH ROW pendant glaring

against the black backdrop like the tunnel
               of light we supposedly see before we die.
I read your work out loud. Soon,

all eyes are on me—then, on you:
               the resilient rose that grew from concrete.
Dear 2Pac, this generation that needs Ritalin

& iPods to focus holds their ears of glass
               against your poems & eavesdrops.
Dear 2Pac, Daniel, the youngblood

chilling in the back, cracks open my copy
               of your book. He admires the page the way
he admires his Cool Grey Jordans.

Dear 2Pac, Daniel, who yesterday refused
               to copy notes on enjambment
& end-stopped lines, handwrites your longest

poem word for word. Daniel, who's always the first
                    to beg if he can dip out early, begs me to kick
knowledge on where he can cop your book.

Dear 2Pac, you real cool: not 'cause you died
                    soon; not 'cause you thinned gin
with juice but 'cause you've transformed

apathetic adolescents into military-
                    minded soldiers ready to unlock
their imaginations off safety.

Regulate

That guy's a rapper; I don't know why he's on this slide.
—A MILITARY RECRUITER, 2014

The S.Sgt. speaking
        to my students
has my homie

Nate Dogg hemmed
        up in a garbage PowerPoint.

Fails to recognize
        he held it down
for the Marines.

A munitions specialist,
        whose soulful singing

had more swerve
        than a cruise missile.
Long Beach legend,

three years departed,
        enlisted in the Corps

to become a man
who'd command respect
but gets dissed

by one of his own. Laid
        back like a G-funk

track, I point at the glossy
          brochure of brotherhood,
containing massive propaganda,

& challenge the S.Sgt.'s strongest
          recruit to fold it into thirds.

Ronda Final (Already)

OutKast Crown

after Patricia Smith

OutKast, rocking tight plaits beneath Braves caps,
spit Southernplayalisticadillac flows
that equated the rap game with selling snow.
They put the Dirty South on the map:
East Point, College Park, ATL to be exact.
In '94, Rebel flags still flapped from trucks for show.
Big Boi & Dre waxed poetic on Jim Crow,
rhyming over groovy bass & turntable scratch.
'Kast kicked knowledge that stuck like grits to fish,
like seasonal pollen to a windshield.
Never worried about whether nighttime would yield
groupie coochie. Took soul sisters on trips
to the dungeon for some Afrocentric loving. The joy
of arranging orgasms into organized noise.

Arranging orgasms into organized noise
was something I knew nothing about,
but I knew I was an outcast with much clout.
As payback for calling me *Boy*
& parading racist lawn jockeys like toys,
I bumped "Ain't No Thang" on my block so loud
the white liberals became Republicans. Proud-
ly, 'Kast didn't subdue racial emotion. Devoid
of tolerance they were. Wrote critical
commentary that skewered raw hypocrisy
& injustice. Realized true democracy
was contained like day-old bacon fat. Cynical,
a word preachers dumped in backseats,
rode shotgun when Whitewalls screeched.

Riding shotgun as Whitewalls screeched,
I wanted to wage war with New York
for booing OutKast at the Source Awards.
The South got somethin' to say. Capiche?
Booty Shake era was squashed, unlike the beef
I had that was so silly it could've passed for pork.
The awards presenters should've handed out forks
because it looked like hip-hop was done, Chief.
The line Suge Knight drew in the sand
stretched longer than the Mason-Dixon.
Dartise deemed Death Row Records was tripping.
Another Civil War would demand
the lives of two four-star generals at their best,
but in this clash North & South held Peace to its chest.

The North & the South held Peace to its chest,
but Big Boi & Dre still felt alienation
echo like reggae reverb. Their elevation
above rap's thematic of lobby-level pimp fests
& gun shop talk made the South doubt their success.
Losing fair-weather fans meant no devastation
for two dope boys who'd already rocked the nation—
their career, on the rise like Southern cess.
Didn't want to float face down in the mainstream;
"L.A." Reid granted them more creative control
to express the minimalist aesthetic they extolled.
An extraterrestrial feel beamed
with secular soul invading gospel organ riffs
& lyrics as complex as cursive hieroglyphs.

With spacey lyrics as complex as hieroglyphs,
'Kast hovered atop hip-hop's pyramid.
ATLiens wasn't a failed experiment;
it enabled Big Boi & Dre to showcase their gift,

but several critics spun adrift
like astronauts. Became lost in a myriad
of deep metaphors that explored serious
themes—Andre 3000's drastic shift
from smoking spliffs to catching natural highs
freestyling over sparse instrumentals
& Big Boi's musings on gaining credentials
as a father caught everyone by surprise:
Mmmmmeeeee & Yooooouuuuu,
Yo Mama & Yo cousin, too.

My mama & my female cousins, too, were glad
my Guess jeans stopped sagging like Spanish moss,
but when the complexion of the man nailed to the cross
came into question no one overstood but 'Kast.
Must have been difficult for them not to brag
about how rap's vegetation, which grew nonstop
in shady places, pointed them in the right spot
while the mind states of haters tended to drag
like the tangled magnetic tape of cassettes.
To Realness, they displayed diligent devotion
the way women keep tabs on their lover's Trojans.
Portraying fraudulent fortune was taboo like Death
appearing in a rusty, jacked-up hooptie ride
that would force Jesus to enter the passenger door to drive.

Forcing Jesus to enter the passenger door to drive
a battered Brougham proves Death is as funny as God.
Not fearing growing old isn't considered odd
when you & your high school homie revive
Southern rap music's status like Lazarus. Alive
& well. No Witchdoctor's help from the DF squad.
Just a Decatur psalm to make heads nod.

Their verbal virtuosity I imbibed
from a landmark album that pushed
the envelope & stamped it with relevant
postage that's honored to this day—excellent
for the hardcore fan, not the corporate crook
who expected the same ole OutKast
to continue rocking tight plaits beneath Braves caps.

Unsung

My mama hated rap, but I came home
from Pryor Middle School one day & found
a Camelot Music bag hanging at the end
of a banister: inside, Geto Boys's *We Can't Be Stopped*:
a tape I'd coveted for weeks. Maybe her mind
was playing tricks on her because the album
cover featured Bushwick Bill holding an ice pack
to soothe the bullet lodged in his eye—
Willie D & Scarface, the other rap crew
members, flanking the gurney on opposite sides.

I was amazed the song entitled "Gotta Let
Your Nuts Hang" didn't induce a grand mal
seizure. "If that song's about what I think . . ."
"No, mama, *Gotta let your nuts hang*
is a 5th Ward Houston expression meaning
having the balls to say *No*": as in when the CEO
of your record label notices your right eye hanging
out of your socket & sees that as an opportune
time to snap a group photo that would cement
your status as being realer than "Real Deal" Holyfield.

Geto Boys were real: not in the sense
that they'd blast the first fool who looked
at them sideways but because their most famous
track was so personal it made me believe
they'd expressed a drug dealer's private thoughts:
fleeting moments of paranoia & suicidal ideations
written on pages of yellow legal pad paper
the music industry kept tucked
beneath bulletproof vests—the contrast
of what was considered primo product.

Houston

Where cookies & cream custom-painted Impalas
sit on full-moon-inch rims. Where DJ Screw
transformed tongue-twisting lyrics into slurred/
slurred/ slurred/ so-so lilo qu-qu quies
that muh/ muh/ muh moved/ moved s-s-s-s-slower/
slower than the elixir of purple drank poured into Styrofoam.
Where the disturbing air of menace hitchhikes
across tollways. Where muthasuckas be squeezed
limes steady on the grind. Where drop-top aggression
lowers property value. Where the exposed flesh
of downtown buildings are tinted red from sunburn.
Where The Ghost of Enron audits Business Ethics
classes. Where the press media blacked-out
the gospel of desegregated lunch counters.

Where allergy forecasts report high levels of ragweed
rebellion. Where pigeons toss bread crusts to politicians.
Where rain is an estranged mother. Where cats clock
relief-pitcher speed on interstates. Where cops claim
they come in peace when descending
into residential war zones. Where hot sauce enjoys
being the life of the party. Where local rap stars
refuse to explode & become supernova sellouts.

Olympic Butter Gold (Havana, Cuba Interlude)

the speaker is Fab 5 Freddy

Representing Cuba in the Freestyle Battle
Event is Telmary who cuts

down her opponents like sugarcane.
The phrase "¡Que equivocao"

spray-painted in white bubble
letters across her orange headwrap

could be a jab against misogynistic
mic fiends who believe female MCs

should keep their feminist salt & pepa
spice hidden in the pantry.

Could be an implicit diss
against President Obama's

camp. Some say if America wins
the gold, it would be epic

poetic justice if Assata Shakur
suddenly appeared in the camera's

field of view & stood
behind the medalist

at the precise moment
the picture is snapped.

Hip-Hop

after Yasiin Bey (FKA Mos Def)

Hip-Hop escaped a Jersey prison
& received political asylum in Cuba,

is on hunger strike until Guantánamo
Bay complies with Geneva Conventions.

Hip-Hop's survived codeine
overdoses but be strung out on Oxy.

Hip-Hop's a firefighter rescuing
gospel rap from burning black churches.

Hip-Hop's turning blood money
into flood disaster relief,

seeks sole custody
of all the stars & spacecrafts

chasing comets composed
of ready rock.

Hip-Hop's dropped from planetary
status to dwarf planet madness:

too small to clear Cristal
bottles out of its path. Hip-Hop's

the first female to make the FBI's
Most Wanted Terrorists List.

Pintata

for Diego Felipe Becerra

You were a feline without whiskers,
unable to sense danger approaching.
Your spray paint gave Felix the Cat
Life the moment a cop snuffed yours.

Now, in Bogotá, Liberal Guilt sanctions
Street Art as long as cats bomb
graffiti that attracts tourists like mice.
The mayor, pulling artistic integrity apart
like string cheese, tries keeping pintatas
from popping up in undesignated zones
so the memory of your foul death
remains buried in litter boxes.

Diego, before your spirit escaped
from your body like mist from a can,
Bogotá's buildings were seen as furniture—
& graffiti, unnecessary scratch marks.

If only the cop knew
your incessant clawing
stemmed from the biological
need to stay sharp.

2084 (From Ghetto Fabulous to Ghetto Fascist)

Niggas are prohibited
from playing dominoes;

the only mathematics
niggas study is subtraction.

Any nigga suspected
of knowing addition

will be buried alive
inside the equals sign.

The only doo process
niggas need to be concerned

with is his or her perm.
There are nigga checkpoints

at every barbershop. All niggas
should be prepared to two-step

& pop their collars on command.
If nigga wallflowers think they're too cool

to entertain live audiences,
we will wipe their brains & implant

a fake fondness
for shucking & jiving.

If these niggas uproot suppressed memories
of shock therapy & chemical castration,

we'll use pennies to exfoliate
their skin: enough times

until their subconscious connects
the humiliating act of tossing their bodies

into a fountain to that of a majestic
wish come true. Any niggas using martial

arts to roundhouse kick martial law
will be shrunken down to subatomic

particles & be displaced in the labyrinth
of another nigga's cornrows.

2Pac Pantoum

Against all odds
Stay true.
It ain't easy
Under pressure.

Stay true.
Hold on. Be strong.
Under pressure,
Keep ya head up.

Hold on. Be strong.
Life goes on.
Gotta keep your head up
Young black male

'Cause life goes on.
I ain't mad at cha.
Young black male,
Holler at me.

I ain't mad at cha.
Heaven ain't hard to find.
Holler at me.

Heaven ain't hard to find.
The streets are death row.
Lord knows
The good die young.

The streets are death row.
It ain't easy.
The good die young.
You must survive against all odds.

2084 (Remix)

Niggas may perceive themselves as fly,
but they'll never have a nest egg.

Gothic Barkley

for Avery Langston Erumuse Moody

In that black & white Nike commercial,
I saw Barkley as a gargoyle perched
on the low-post block: both elbows, extended

like wings, ready to box out Responsibility
for hurling profanity as stale as popcorn.

Barkley confessed he wasn't *paid*
to be a role model, but twenty-plus years
later, I see Gothic Barkley as a lookout

encouraging boys to peer through the glamour
of popping championship champagne

& see the NBA for what it truly is: a place
where McDonald's High School All-Americans
who've started every game since sixth grade

will be exceptional enough to have twelfth
man status on a pro team giving only nine dudes

playing time, exceptional enough
to have less marketing value than a mascot.
Avery, by the time you see the ad,

the whole desolate gym aura, the black & white
cinematography intense as Gothic Barkley's grunts

& the rebounds he snatches with authority,
you might find the imagery annoying like the constant

sneaker squeaks you hear in the background.

Here's the intimidating truth: my father retired
from the air force as a major, but if he got *paid to dunk*

a basketball & wreak havoc on the court,
I might've ignored his verbal abuse like a referee.
Think of this poem as a late, late whistle.

Parents should be role models,
but Gothic Barkley wanted to say more:

that just because the head of my household
refuses to man up, I shouldn't expect Nikes
to transform him into *Time* magazine's Father of the Year.

But Nike wouldn't have approved
that message; it's too gloomy:

scarier than a Victorian novel about how lightening
can bring the dead back to life but can't resurrect
a decaying relationship between father & son.

If poetry can achieve what one hundred
million watts of electricity can't,

by the time you read this piece, your granddad
& I will have ended our seven-year silence.
Son, no matter how much our bond

might decompose, from my end,
the stench won't smell as bad as mold.

Even if your shoe size is bigger than eleven
& a half, make sure you address me
by the same title given to Barkley: "Sir."

Notes

The opening quote from Chuck D appears in his essay "Open Letter on Media, Messages & Pimps," originally published in 2011 at http://www.allhiphop.com.

"Son of a": The poem includes lyrics from Augustus Pablo's dub instrumental "King Tubby Meets Uptown Rockers."

"Mr. Señor Love Daddy": The poem includes a refrain from Crime Mob's song "Knuck if You Buck".

"Telecommunications Act of 1996, or Ode to Black Radio": The poem is inspired by Clinton's decision to deregulate radio station ownership. Lyrics are from "Kiss" by Prince and from "How I Could Just Kill a Man" by Cypress Hill.

"Bricolage": The poem is partly inspired by the 1983 PBS documentary on hip-hop culture called *Style Wars*, directed by Tony Silver.

"The Low End Theory": The poem is a contrapuntal and should be read in the following order: read the title as the first line, then read from the top of the left-hand column to the bottom of the left-hand column, and from the top of the right-hand column to the bottom. Reread the title again as the first line, and read across the margins: zigzag all the way down from the left-hand column to the right-hand column.

"Luke Cage, Hip-Hop Superhero for Hire": The poem is inspired by *Blank Panther*, no. 14: "Bride of the Panther, Part 1." Reginald Hudlin (writer), Scot Eaton (pencils), and Klaus Janson (inks). Marvel Comics, March 22, 2006.

"What's Beef: The Unauthorized Biography of Dr. Henry Irons's Alter Ego, Steel": The poem is inspired by *Steel*, vol. 2, no. 0: "In the Beginning!" Louise Simonson (writer), Chris Batista (pencils), and Rich Faber (inks). DC Comics, October 1, 1994.

"Supersonic": The title of the poem comes from J. J. Fad's song.

"Lovelust à la Mode": This poem contains lyrics from "Ice Cream" by Wu-Tang Clan.

"Olympic Butter Gold (United States East Coast Interlude)": The poem contains lyrics from Wu-Tang Clan's song "Triumph."

"Kleosphobia": Kleosphobia is a word the author invented. "Kleos" derives from the Greek for "renown" or "glory." Kleosphobia, then, means the fear of losing one's glory (i.e., street cred).

"Ersatz": The poem includes a refrain from Luke's song "I Wanna Rock."

"The Thief's Theme": The title of the poem comes from Nas's song.

"Dear 2Pac,": Toward the end, the poem contains phrases from Gwendolyn Brooks's poem "We Real Cool."

"Regulate": The title of the poem comes from Warren G's song "Regulate," featuring Nate Dogg.

"OutKast Crown": The poem is inspired by Patricia Smith's heroic sonnets "Motown Crown" and contains lyrics from "Elevators" by OutKast.

"Unsung": The poem is inspired by the *TV One* documentary series *Unsung*, "The Geto Boys" episode. November 13, 2013.

"Pintata": The poem is loosely inspired by Sergio Elmir's article "Justin Bieber's 'Graffiti' Is All Ego, No Art." *Huffington Post: The Blog*, November 6, 2013.

"2Pac Pantoum": With the exception of the first half of the last line, each line includes a 2Pac song title.